D1609580

The Story of
The Totem Pole

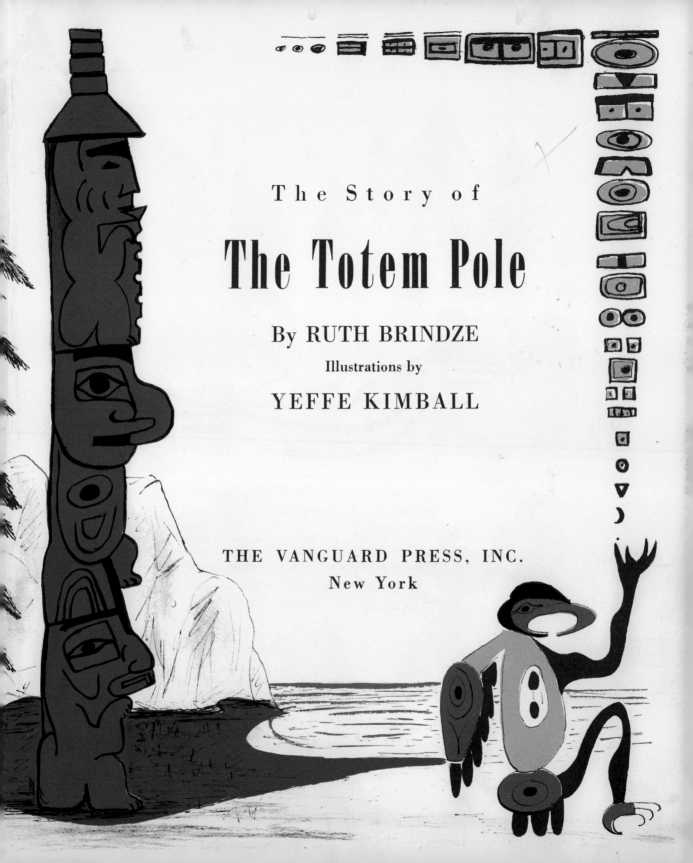

The Story of
The Totem Pole

By RUTH BRINDZE

Illustrations by

YEFFE KIMBALL

THE VANGUARD PRESS, INC.
New York

Contents

The Storytelling Poles

THE Indians who lived long ago on the American Northwest coast and near the rivers that flow into the Pacific Ocean had a wonderful way of recording their stories: they carved them on poles.

These decorated trees — totem poles we call them — were carved with strange and beautiful figures, representing real people, animals, birds, and fish, as well as imaginary creatures, and each one illustrates some story or part of a story.

Why did the Northwest coast Indians carve their stories on trees? One answer is that this was a convenient way to record them. The Indians had no alphabet like ours, and so did not write as we do, but they were skilled woodworkers, and where these tribes lived (in the coastal regions from southern Alaska to the north tip of California), there were thick, dark forests in which red cedar trees grew to gigantic heights. These forest giants made perfect poles for carving, and therefore, when someone wished to record a tale, it was illustrated on a tree. The Indians who lived on the plains, where there are no trees, painted pictures of their legends on their tepees, and other tribes wove story designs into blankets and baskets. But the Northwest coast Indians used cedar poles for most of their storytelling records.

No one can say exactly when these Indians started to carve totem poles nor how the first one happened to be made. According to one account, the first carved pole was found on a beach after a great storm, and the people thought it so beautiful that they decided to make others

7

like it. After many copies had been made, someone carved a pole with different figures, and then, as time went on, trees were decorated with illustrations of many favorite legends.

This is one explanation of how totem-pole carving started, and it is quite possible that a decorated pole actually was carried by winds and ocean currents to the American coast from one of the Pacific islands, where the people were also expert wood carvers. But even though there is some mystery about the first totem poles, we do know a great deal about the poles of the Northwest Indians — how they were chosen, transported, and carved, and what stories the figures illustrated.

Some totem poles record the legends of a tribe or of a chief's personal adventures, and some poles commemorate one special event or the memory of a person. There also were "ridicule" poles that were put up to embarrass someone who had failed to pay a debt, had failed to keep a promise, or had done something else wrong.

The men who were the most skillful carvers made a specialty of decorating poles, and they traveled from one village to another to fill orders from chiefs and other important persons. Totem-pole artists were well paid for their work, and in addition to this expenditure a pole owner was expected to celebrate the completion of the pole with a big party that might last for several weeks, or even for several months. Adding it all together, having your own totem pole was costly, yet some men and women had more than one pole; a new one might be ordered to tell about a recent victory or adventure, or merely because the owner thought his old pole looked shabby.

The stories carved on a pole were always recited at the big party given to celebrate its erection, and they were retold on other occasions. In the

8

retelling, certain details of a tale might be varied, since each person recounted it in his own words and as he remembered it, but few changes were made in the important parts. A father telling his son a story that he had heard from his father would naturally change, add, or omit certain facts. But the figures on the pole — the illustrations of the story — reminded him of the main theme.

Because totem-pole stories were passed along from one person to another, most poles still can be "read"; that is, the story can be paired up with the carving. But there are puzzle poles whose stories have been forgotten, and, since the Indians usually did not make their figures look true to life, it is sometimes impossible to guess exactly what the carving represents.

Long ago, when only a few white men had explored the Northwest coast, the captain of one ship was asked to assist in putting up a pole. This event was noted in the ship's log, or diary, but even men who worked on the pole were not certain whether the carved figure was a toad or a bear! Yet they found the experience thrilling, and so will you as you read about the pole with the single carved figure on top, and about others decorated from top to bottom with curious and fascinating carvings.

Captain Roberts Does a Favor

A LADIES' dressmaker — that's what I've become," complained Stitches the sailmaker.

Some sailors who were watching their shipmate cut old sails into skirts and blouses nodded sympathetically. But Jack, the tease, picked up one of the skirts, slipped it on, and proceeded to do a little dance.

10

"Maybe you should keep this one for your Missus," he said, patting the coarse cloth. "What a fine gift it will make after all the years you've been away."

Everyone laughed but Stitches, who grumbled, "The Indians like them."

Nearly four years before, on a gray November morning in 1791, the schooner "Jefferson" had sailed out of Boston on a fur-trading voyage. She had rounded Cape Horn, the southerly tip of South America, and after a few stops to replenish water and food supplies, had headed for the Northwest Pacific coast. Now the ship was anchored between two islands off the west coast of Canada.

Stitches had been ordered to make clothes out of spare sails because, after several years of trading, there were no more goods left on board that could be bartered. All the iron tools, all the cloth and trinkets that had been brought from Boston, had been traded for furs, but Chief Cunneah's great storehouse was still filled with sea otters and other valuable skins, and, in order to get them, Captain Josiah Roberts needed something the Indians would take in exchange. So he had put Stitches to work making clothing, and Chips, as a ship's carpenter was usually called, was busy making chests which were to be carried ashore and traded for furs.

Soon after Jack had finished his little dance, Captain Roberts looked out of the doorway of his cabin and saw two Indians paddling toward his ship. As the canoe drew closer, Captain Roberts recognized the paddlers as the two oldest nephews of Chief Cunneah, and he surmised, since the messengers were of high rank, that their mission was important. When the messengers climbed to the deck of the schooner, the Captain was

11

waiting to greet them, and soon he heard the reason they had come. Chief Cunneah was planning to erect a totem pole, and he asked whether the white brothers would come to the village to help.

Captain Roberts was delighted at being asked to do a favor, for he wanted to make a real friend of Chief Cunneah, both because it might make fur trading easier and because altogether it was better to be on good terms with the Indians.

The Chief's nephews were given biscuits and pudding, and Captain Roberts promised he would start for the village as soon as possible. He told Chips to pack all the tools that might be needed and to see that Timothy, his assistant, also was ready. Then he asked the first mate to select the sailors who would row the party ashore.

In the afternoon, when Captain Roberts landed, he saw a great cedar tree on the beach. This was to be smoothed and shaped into a pole which was to be set up in front of Chief Cunneah's house.

Chips and Timothy got to work at once, for there was much to be done before the pole would be ready. Meanwhile some of Chief Cunneah's men were digging a big hole in which the pole was to stand.

The Chief, who came out to welcome the boat party, was about the same height as the Captain, and his skin was about the same color as Josiah Roberts' weather-beaten face. But Cunneah's hair was black, and he wore it shoulder length.

After watching the work for a while, the Chief invited Captain Roberts to go to the storehouse with him, probably because he wanted to show off the many fine skins that were hanging there. And the Captain hoped, as he looked around, that the work his men were doing on the pole would bring payment of at least a few skins.

12

Shortly before dark, the sailors rowed back to their ship, carrying with them a big salmon and a pailful of blueberries that the Indians had given them as gifts. Before leaving, Captain Roberts had promised that his men would come again the next day to help set up the pole.

Everyone on the ship was in good humor that night; the afternoon in Cunneah's village had been an interesting excursion, and the fresh fish and berries made a pleasant change from the dried and salted food that was regularly served. Before turning in for the night, the lucky men who were to go to the village again the next day began to plan the best way to set up the pole.

13

Timothy, who was a boy of about fourteen, asked what Chief Cunneah would have done if the Indians had had to finish and put up the pole themselves.

"They could have managed," said Chips, "but it would have taken much longer. You saw that they had tools for smoothing the tree — 'toes,' they call them. They use these sharp iron blades as we do a chisel. Too bad," he added thoughtfully, "that we have no more iron to trade for furs."

The next day, First Mate Magee went ashore with the men who were to paint and erect the pole. Some spare masts from the ship were used as a derrick to lift the cedar pole into the hole which had been dug in front of Chief Cunneah's house.

The pole stood straight and tall, but it was entirely plain; there was no decoration on it whatsoever. Later on, about three weeks after the great wooden column was erected, the Indians fastened a carving onto the top of the pole. First Officer Magee thought it looked like a toad, but another sailor said that it was supposed to represent a bear. The figure and the pole were painted a brick red, and the teeth, eyes, nostrils, and the insides of the ears of the animal were made of the beautiful abalone shell. Even though the men from Boston could not decide what the figure was supposed to be, they all agreed that it was beautiful.

But Chief Cunneah did not wait until the figure was fastened atop the pole to give his celebration party. The night after the pole was put up, the chief and his wife invited the American sailors to attend the celebration.

"This is going to be a real potlatch," said Captain Roberts when he received the invitation. "We are all going to have a wonderful time."

14

The Potlatch or Giveaway Party

CAPTAIN ROBERTS and his men were the first guests to arrive for the celebration, but soon afterward three big dugout canoes filled with Indians from a nearby village approached the landing beach. Then a strange thing happened. When only a few yards from shore, the paddlers stopped, and a man in the first canoe, who was the chief of the visiting Indians, picked up a bundle of thin strips of wood and one by one dropped the wooden pieces into the water. After throwing in the last one, he said:

"By your invitation, we have traveled a very long distance from home, and these sticks represent the amount of goods we received from you a while back. We return the same amount with interest, two for one."

Now Chief Cunneah made a speech of welcome, and when it was finished, the canoes were paddled onto the beach, and as the visitors stepped out each one was greeted by Chief Cunneah and his wife. Then the American sailors were introduced to the new arrivals.

The program began with songs sung by everyone except the sailors from the schooner "Jefferson," who did not know either the words or the music. Then a girl came from behind a curtain made of blankets, and she walked backwards, slowly and gracefully, toward the singing people. One of the elders of the tribe was waiting to receive her, and when she reached him, a new song was started. Then, while everyone watched, the girl's lower lip was slit with a small, sharp instrument so that she could wear a labret, which is a thin piece of wood or bone that the Northwest coast women thought made them look handsome. There were three other girls who had their lips slit; two were quite small, but all went through the ceremony bravely and proudly.

After it was over, there was a display of the gifts that had been brought to Chief Cunneah. They were carried around so that everyone had a chance to look at them. In addition to the dresses and chests brought by the American sailors, there were war clothes made of moose skins, shawls and blankets woven of strips of cedar bark, furs, and many copper and iron ornaments.

"It's a good haul," said Captain Roberts, "but if I were Cunneah, I doubt that I would look so happy about the gifts. You see, when he's invited to a potlatch by the visiting chief, Cunneah is going to have to bring twice as many gifts as he has received."

16

"So that's what the visiting chief meant when he spoke of returning two for one," the first mate murmured.

Then he learned more about the etiquette of potlatching. The name "potlatch" comes from the Indian words *pat shotl,* which means "giving." At these special parties, which were held to celebrate the completion of a new totem pole or a new house, or some other important event, the guests were expected to bring twice as many gifts as their host had brought to them at some previous celebration. The public display of these gifts enabled the chief to know the wealth of his tribe.

Actually, gift giving was the banking system of the Northwest coast Indians. Instead of putting money in a savings account, as we do today, they gave valuable articles to relatives or neighbors, with the expectation of being paid back with interest at some later date.

However, since each village had at least one potlatch every year, you can understand that this custom created problems, for the number and the value of the gifts that had to be produced kept increasing and increasing. As time went on, many people had to go into debt in order to obtain enough gifts, and often they gave back presents that had been given to them, in addition to bringing new things. No one would think of doing this today, but the Indians of the Northwest coast were not offended when a guest brought back a present.

Yet, even though the guests brought valuable gifts, giving a potlatch was an expensive affair. First of all, the host usually had to provide vast quantities of food, for guests usually had to make long journeys to reach the party, and it was natural that they wanted to stay and visit a while before starting the trip back home. A potlatch therefore might continue for several days, weeks, or even months.

17

Furthermore, each guest had to be given a gift — and not an inexpensive souvenir but something that was really valuable. At some potlatches the host and hostess gave away practically everything they and their relatives owned, in order to impress their guests with their generosity.

When Chief Cunneah began to give out his presents, each person seemed pleased with what he received. The gifts were distributed according to the guest's importance; the visiting chief and the elders were given theirs first, and, of course, they got the best presents. Captain Roberts received exactly the gift he had hoped for: a beautiful sea-otter skin that he had often admired. Other valuable furs were then presented to First Mate Magee, to Chips and to his assistant, Timothy, who had helped with the pole, and to other sailors from the schooner "Jefferson."

Timothy had signed up for the voyage as an apprentice, and therefore he did not expect to be paid much in wages. When Cunneah gave him the skin, he was especially happy, for Timothy guessed that the fur could be sold for as much money as he would draw from the ship for the entire voyage.

After all the presentations had been made, Cunneah's wife stepped forward. She waited for a moment until she had everyone's full attention and then began to speak in a low voice.

"The Chief has received many fine gifts, and I, as well as he, thank you for them. But I have something very special to give him — a present I'm sure he'll enjoy. Here it is!"

She handed Cunneah a bulky bundle which turned out to be an old blanket raveled at one end and torn at the other. Since it was customary to play jokes at a potlatch, no one was surprised, but everyone, including Cunneah, laughed when the ragged blanket was displayed.

The laughing stopped suddenly when someone blew a loud whistle and six young men rushed out from behind one of the houses. Each one wore a mask, some made to look like birds' heads, with beaks and feathers, and others like the heads of animals. As the young men ran toward the guests, drums were beaten and everyone seemed to be making as much noise as possible. The young men wearing the masks then began to dance; each one danced alone, some spinning around rapidly and others moving with slow, graceful steps.

This dance was followed by another performed by the masked group of the visiting Indians, who affected the manners and gestures of the birds and animals they represented.

After the dancing, the feasting began. There was deer, bear, and seal meat, roasted waterfowl, whale tidbits, and chunks of salmon. For dessert, there were fresh wild blueberries and currants. The food was served in huge wooden vessels carved and shaped to look like animals, fish, and people. The meat and fish were cut into small pieces, each one just about a mouthful. The guests were not given separate dishes, but each person dipped his spoon into the big serving bowl, which was about ten feet long. However, Cunneah apologized that the dish was no larger. Some chiefs, he said, had serving vessels that measured twenty, thirty, or even forty feet. The visiting Indians had brought along their own spoons, and the American sailors were lent spoons by Cunneah's wife.

The feasting continued for a long time, and, even though everyone had been hungry and ate a good deal, there was a tremendous quantity of food left over. Cunneah and his wife knew that there would be, but if they had prepared any less, their visitors would have thought that they were not being sufficiently generous.

About a month after the potlatch, Captain Roberts made ready to sail for home, for the ship had a full cargo of valuable furs, all carefully cleaned and stowed. When these were sold, the Captain and many of the other sailors who were to collect a percentage of the profits at the end of the voyage would be rich men. Some never went to sea again, and others, who had had enough of long voyages, would not sign on ships bound for the Northwest coast. But Timothy made another of these long passages, and on this trip he was the ship's carpenter.

Through the Toad

On his second voyage to the Northwest coast, Timothy frequently spoke of the pole he had helped the Indians erect and of the potlatch that had been given to celebrate when the pole was put up. Even though many years had passed since the party at Chief Cunneah's, the carpenter recalled every detail of the event, and he hoped that on this voyage he would be lucky enough to be invited by the Indians to another celebration.

When the boat was steered toward land, Timothy climbed to the top of the mainmast so that from this vantage point he would be the first to see Cunneah's village. For a long while he remained aloft, seeing nothing but thick forests, and, above, blue sky and wispy clouds. Finally he caught a glimpse of a clearing in the forest and of the big rectangular houses in which the Northwest coast Indians lived. Then he saw the pole, the one with the bear at the top, on which he had worked. As soon as he spied it, he knew the houses were Cunneah's village; for him, just as for the Indians when they traveled over land or on the ocean, the pole was a landmark. It guided them to the village.

By the time the boat was anchored and everything had been made shipshape, it was too late to go ashore, but the next morning Timothy went in with the first landing party. Cunneah did not recognize the carpenter, which was not surprising, since Tim had been only a boy when last he had been in the village. But the carpenter remembered enough words of Cunneah's language to remind him of the bear pole and of the potlatch, and soon the Chief was acting like an old friend.

"If only you had arrived a little earlier," said Cunneah regretfully, "you would have seen a bigger, better potlatch than the one I gave. A new house was built nearby, and the chief gave the greatest feast I have ever attended."

Cunneah then described the house, and as he told about it, Tim became more and more curious. Fortunately, Cunneah had planned to make a trip to the village to visit relatives, and he invited the carpenter to accompany him.

They traveled in a canoe made of a cedar log that had been scooped out so that only a thin shell of the wood remained. The canoe was sharply pointed at both ends, and it was paddled by two of Cunneah's slaves — Indians captured in battle whom Cunneah had brought back to work for him.

There were eight houses in the village; the new one was the most prominent, not merely because it was the biggest but because there was a carved pole that was attached to the house. Unlike Cunneah's pole, which had only a single figure on top, this one had animals and human figures carved from the very top to the bottom of the pole. The bottom figure was a toad, and to enter the house you walked right through the toad. The house looked impressive from the outside; it was oblong in shape,

about sixty feet long, thirty feet wide, and twenty feet high. It had a slanting roof, similar to those built today, but it had no chimney. The smoke went out through a hole in the roof.

The interior of the house proved to be even more interesting than the outside. In the center of the big room was a large bare place where a fire was burning. All the families who lived in this community house used this fireplace to do their cooking, and it was also used to heat the building.

At the far end of the room were two carved posts that supported the roof beams, which were heavy, round cedar logs; and the carvings on both poles were the same. The top carving was of a man, and the bottom one was of an animal that Timothy thought was a seal. Later, when he heard the story of the carvings, he learned that the animal actually was a sea lion, even though the figure did not look like the real sea lions one sees in the zoo.

Cunneah's relative, who was also a chief, lived in the space just in back of the carved house posts. This location was usually chosen by a chief for his living quarters, possibly because it was the most comfortable part of the house, since it was farthest from the front door. The chief's sister, whose oldest son, according to this tribe's custom, would succeed his uncle and be the next chief, lived in an adjoining space with her family. Each of the families who lived in the house had its own quarters, separated, one from another, by screening, and you could judge a family's importance by how close its quarters were to the chief's. The slaves slept near the toad-door.

Hanging from the roof were smoked meat and fish, and strings of food were also stretched from one wall of the house to the other. There was such a bountiful supply that all the Sea Lion people, as they were called because their house was named the Sea Lion house, would have plenty to eat even if no fresh food were obtained for a long time.

A big meal was served to the visitors, and Timothy thought the smoked salmon particularly delicious. It was after they had dined that the carpenter learned the reason for Cunneah's visit to his relative; Cunneah wanted to inquire about the man who had carved the posts in the new house — the ones that had attracted Timothy.

28

Although most of the Northwest coast people were skillful carvers, there were a few whose work was outstanding and who specialized in carving totem poles. If a chief wanted a pole, he would choose one of these artists and hire him to do the work. A popular carver, however, often had so many orders that a chief might have to wait a year or more before his pole was started.

Cunneah's questions about the carved posts gave Timothy an opportunity to ask about the figures of the man and the animal. He wanted to know if there were any story connected with them.

"Of course, there is a story," said his host. "It is about one of my people, and I will gladly tell it — that is, if Cunneah, who knows it well, does not mind hearing it again."

Cunneah said that he would be glad to hear the tale, and so the story of Black-Skin and the sea lion was begun:

Black-Skin was the youngest nephew of a great chief who, while on a hunting expedition, was killed by a bull sea lion. Everyone belonging to the chief's clan vowed vengeance on the sea lions; they would go to the sea lions' rock, they said, and tear the fabulous sea monster in two.

The men then began to train for the expedition — that is, everyone but Black-Skin. Each morning at sunrise they plunged into the cold sea, and then, to test their strength, they tried to pull a limb from a certain tree near the beach. Black-Skin (this was his nickname because he stayed so close to the fire that his skin was blackened with soot) refused to bathe in the icy ocean or to test his strength. Everyone made fun of him, yet Black-Skin did not seem to mind. But his mother was ashamed, and when Black-Skin saw how unhappy she was, he promised that he also would go into training. It was agreed that he would train in secret and that the others in the clan were not to be told of what he was doing.

When his older brothers dived into the ocean, Black-Skin remained by the fire. He bathed at night, when everyone else was asleep, and each night he grew stronger and could remain in the water a little longer. One night he heard a whistle, and he thought that his secret had been discovered. But the man on the beach was a stranger dressed in a bear-skin, who said, "I am Strength. Come and wrestle with me."

The stranger was smaller than Black-Skin, but he quickly threw him to the ground.

30

"You are not strong enough yet," he declared. "I will return and test you again." After saying this, he disappeared.

The next time Black-Skin wrestled with Strength, his grip was so powerful that Strength immediately said there was no need to continue. Then Strength told him to try to pull the limb from the tree. Black-Skin did this easily, and then, as Strength directed, he put the limb back again so that no one would know how powerful he was.

Black-Skin was ready to go on the expedition against the sea lions, but everyone laughed when he asked for a place in the canoe. However, one of his relatives took pity on him and said he could bail water from the canoe on the way to the sea lions' rock, and he was given a place.

The sea lions seemed to know that the men had come to kill them, and they tried to prevent the fighters from landing on the slippery rock. Finally the oldest nephew of the slain chief, who was considered the strongest by everyone, jumped on the rock, but the bull sea lion killed him with a single blow of his flippers. Then the second oldest nephew sprang to the rock, but he also was killed.

After this happened, everyone but Black-Skin was frightened and wanted to paddle away. But Black-Skin leaped from the canoe, picked up the monster by the tail, and tore him in two. Thus Black-Skin became a hero, and when he returned to his village he was made the chief.

When the carpenter returned to his ship after his visit to Cunneah's relatives he told the story of Black-Skin and described the carvings on the posts in the Sea Lion house. Later, some of Timothy's shipmates saw the carved posts and, since they knew the story, the carved figures were not at all puzzling; they recognized Black-Skin and the sea lion.

The Tree Hunt

THERE was great excitement in Cunneah's house when he said that he had chosen the artist who was to carve his new totem pole. From early morning until late at night the pole was discussed — how it should be decorated, when the hunt for a suitable tree should begin, and so on. Timothy's opinion was asked on several occasions, and when preparations were being made for the tree hunt, he was invited to accompany the Indian scouts.

Only a few days after they left Cunneah's village, one of the scouts walked deep into the forest, and near a little lake he saw a tree that would have pleased the Chief. But there was no practical way of carrying it out of the forest and down to the shore. So the scouts traveled on, searching for a big red cedar growing near enough to the ocean's edge so that after it was cut it could be rolled down the beach and into the water.

There were no roads in the Northwest country, and the only convenient means of travel, or of moving things, was by water. The Indians had big canoes that could carry many passengers in addition to freight, and they also had smaller canoes that were more easily paddled and yet were really seaworthy boats. This was the type in which the scouts were traveling.

People frequently say that if you keep on looking and looking for something, you are bound to find it, and that is just what happened on the tree hunt. After much searching, the Indian scouts found a fine red cedar near the shore and quickly went to work cutting it down. When the branches had been removed, several of the men began to scoop the wood from one side of the trunk, just as if they were going to make a canoe.

33

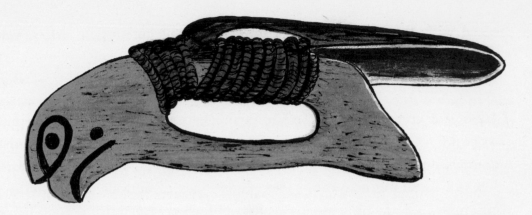

The scouts could have waited to hollow out the tree until it had been brought back to the village, but a hollow tree trunk is naturally lighter in weight and therefore easier to handle than a solid one, and since the tree had to be towed behind the canoe for a long distance, the scouts decided that it would be best to lighten it before starting the trip home. Some totem poles were not hollowed out in this way, but the tallest ones usually were, not merely because they were easier to transport but also because they could be handled more conveniently when the time came to erect them. Furthermore, only one side of the pole was usually carved; the figures of animals and birds and people were carved on the round side, and the scooped-out side was the back, which was not decorated.

When the scouts were nearing their village, one of them took a short cut through the woods to inform the Chief that he would soon see his pole. The news spread quickly, and everyone was so excited that little work was done that day except in the Chief's house, where a big welcome-home dinner was being prepared.

The men of the scouting mission paddled in proudly, for they knew that even though the Chief had expected them back sooner, he would be pleased with the tree they had found. Kita, the totem-pole artist, was waiting on the beach with the Chief.

Kita knew exactly what figures were to be carved on the pole — what was to be on the top, what in the middle, and what on the bottom — for the Chief had given orders about the stories he wished to have illustrated. Kita thought that beautiful carvings could be made of the legends that had been selected, and he was very happy, for he had just completed a pole he wished he could have changed. An artist who carved a totem pole was never at liberty to select the stories; he was paid to carve the pole as the owner wished.

The first thing Kita did was to mark the pole into sections. In each of these sections there was to be a different figure. Sometimes a chief hired many artists to work on a pole, each to do one figure, but Kita was to carve the entire pole, and he marked it for six figures. Of course, the bottom part, that would be buried in the ground, was not to be carved.

The artist and his assistants began by making a smooth pole of the tree trunk, and then the actual carving was started. Kita used a pattern for some of the figures; for instance, when he carved two big eyes, he copied them from the same pattern so that both eyes would be alike. However, for most of the figures he had neither a pattern nor a design; he just went ahead and cut the wood until he had made a figure he liked.

The top of the pole was carved first, and when that figure was finished, Kita prepared to paint it. He used paints he had made himself; the black paint he had made from charcoal, and the white from baked clamshells. He had mixed a yellow paint by combining a copperish clay with some salmon oil, and he made a very beautiful shade of red from the roots of the various berry bushes.

35

Sometimes the painting was not done until the entire pole had been carved, but Kita decided to color each figure as it was finished, for the Chief was expecting visitors, and the artist wanted the pole to look as beautiful as possible.

The Chief was very pleased when the first carving was completed, and, in accordance with his agreement, he promptly paid for that part of the work. This system of paying as the work progressed was the usual custom, but after the Chief's visitors had complimented the artist enthusiastically, the Chief decided to give Kita a number of additional presents.

Like other totem-pole artists, Kita did not try to make his figures look true to life. Instead, he used identifying marks for each bird, animal, or fish, and everyone familiar with the marks could tell what the carving was meant to be.

For example, kindly Beaver — according to some stories, it was he who taught the Indians how to build houses — can be recognized by his cutting teeth, scaly tail, and by a stick held in his front paws.

Shark's mark was an ugly mouth turned down at the corners and filled with sawlike teeth.

Eagle's beak was carved with a downward curve, whereas Hawk's had a decided hook. And Raven was always carved with a straight beak, or with none at all when the carving illustrated the popular legend of how Raven once lost his beak.

Learning and remembering the identification signs is quite easy, and for the people of the Northwest coast the system was particularly convenient because they had no written language. They did not have to memorize an alphabet nor learn how to spell; they merely had to learn to recognize carved or painted designs.

claw   eye   face   nose   claw

When Indians were traveling and arrived at a strange village, the carvings on the poles helped them to find the house in which they would be most welcome. If the traveler were a member of the Eagle clan, he went to the house with an Eagle atop its pole. The bird with the downward-curving beak was a sign that the people living in the house were members of the same clan as the traveler, for both had the same mascot or guardian spirit. If there was no pole with his mascot on top, the traveler tried to find one with Eagle at the bottom. The figure at the bottom often showed the clan to which the pole owner's wife belonged, and if she were a member of the Eagles, the traveler knew he would be welcome to spend the night with his relatives.

However, the figures were not always arranged in this way; the top carving might be of someone the owner wished to honor, or the figure might be the owner's personal mascot. For instance, one hunter had a figure of a bear carved at the top of his pole because, according to the story, a bear had befriended the hunter when he was lost in the woods.

38

The hunter had lived with the bear in its den, and the animal had generously provided him with food and other comforts. When the Indian finally had returned to his village, he announced that he was adopting the bear as his guardian spirit, and he ordered a totem pole with the figure of a bear carved on top.

A totem pole is always "read" from the top down, or, to be more exact, the stories are told according to the position in which the figures have been carved in the pole.

Anyone who knows this and the identifying signs used by the carvers might say, when looking at a pole, that the first story is about Beaver, and the next one is about Raven, and the next about Shark, Toad. and so on.

But even an expert might not be able to tell the exact story. For totem-pole carvings are like illustrations in a book; they suggest what the story is about but do not supply the details.

Once the stories are known, the carved figures are not at all puzzling. Because Timothy had related the story of Black-Skin to his shipmates, they were able to read the house posts on which the story of the fight with the sea lion was carved. And when they saw a carving of a man struggling with a sea lion on other poles, they recognized it as illustrating Black-Skin's adventure. In other words, the more Indian legends one knows, the easier it is to read a pole.

Some popular legends were carved on many poles, and when, in accordance with the custom, the legend was recounted at a potlatch, the majority of the guests knew the story almost as well as the storyteller.

This was probably true of the legend of how Raven lost his beak, for it was one of the best-liked of all the remarkable adventures of Raven, and it was told, over and over again, whenever a figure of Raven without any beak was carved on a pole.

41

Raven and His Remarkable Adventure

THIS is the story about the trick Raven played on the fisherman and how this remarkable creature lost his beak.

The Raven was no ordinary bird; he had remarkable powers and could change into whatever form he wished. He could change from a bird to a man, and not only could he fly and walk, but, when it suited his convenience, he could swim underwater as fast as any fish.

One day Raven took the form of a man and started to walk through the forest. Probably because he was wearing a long white beard, he looked like an old man, and he walked rather slowly. After a while, Raven began to feel hungry, and he wondered how he could most easily get something to eat. As he was thinking about this, he came to the edge of the forest and saw a village near the beach. Then he saw that many people were fishing for halibut.

In a flash Raven thought up a scheme for stealing food. He dived into the sea, swam below the surface of the water to the spot where the fishermen's hooks were dangling, and he began to gobble the bait. He swam from one hook to another, pulling off the bait, and, each time he did this, the fisherman felt the tug and thought that he had caught a fish. But when the line was pulled in, there was no fish nor any bait.

But Raven worked his trick once too often. When Houskana, the fisherman, felt a tug, he jerked his line quickly and hooked something heavy. But he could not pull in the line. What had happened was this: when Raven tried to steal Houskana's bait, his jaw was caught on the

43

hook, and while the fisherman tugged on his line, Raven pulled in the other direction. Then he held on to some rocks at the bottom of the sea and he cried, "O rocks, please help me." But the rocks would not help. Then, because he was in great pain, he said to his jaw, "Break off, O jaw, for I am tired now." Raven's jaw obeyed, and when it broke off, Houskana felt his line suddenly become free, and he pulled it in quickly. On the hook was a man's jaw with a long beard. It looked horrible enough to scare anyone, and Houskana and the other fishermen were completely frightened, for they thought that the jaw might belong to some evil spirit. So they ran back to the chief's house as fast as they could.

Raven then came from under the water and followed the fishermen. Although he was in great pain because his jaw had broken off, no one could tell that anything was wrong, because he covered the lower part of his face with his blanket.

The people were examining the jaw, which was still hanging on the halibut hook. It was handed from one to another, and finally Raven said, "Give it to me; let me look at it, too."

"Oh, this is a wonder," he exclaimed, and then he threw back his blanket and put his jaw into place.

Raven did this so quickly that the people did not have time to see what was happening. And as soon as his jaw was on again, Raven turned himself into a bird and flew off through the smoke hole of the chief's house. Only then did the people realize that it was Raven, the trickster, who had stolen their bait and who had been hooked on Houskana's line.

When this story is illustrated, Raven is carved not as an old man, for that was just one of many forms that this super-bird had assumed for this particular adventure, but as a bird without a beak.

44

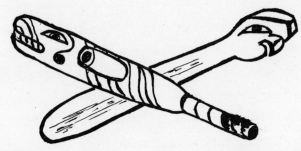

The Fight Over the Tallest Pole

ONE OF THE most famous feuds in the history of totem-pole land resulted from a competition between two rival chiefs, each of whom was determined to have the tallest pole.

Sharp-Teeth was chief of the Eagles, and Sispagut of the Killer-Whales, and whatever one did, the other tried to outdo. This rivalry had been going on for a long time, when Sispagut decided to order a totem pole.

The Killer-Whale chief made sure that his rival was told about the tremendous tall tree that had been cut for his pole, and that he was kept informed about all the preparations. When the famous carver, Oyai, was hired to decorate the pole, Sispagut himself told the news to Sharp-Teeth.

"What an insult to Laderh," shouted Sharp-Teeth.

Laderh was a wood carver who was related to Sispagut and who, according to tribal custom, should have been given the job of decorating the pole. However, his work was not nearly so good as Oyai's. Laderh knew this, yet, to avenge the insult, he plotted with Sharp-Teeth to prevent Sispagut from erecting his tall pole.

45

First, Laderh threatened Sispagut with all sorts of terrible things if the work on the pole were not stopped. But Sispagut merely shrugged his shoulders and said that Oyai would go ahead according to schedule.

"Then cut off some of this 'walking stick,'" ordered the scornful Laderh. "It is not fitting for you to have one so tall."

As far as anyone knew, Sispagut had taken the biggest red cedar tree for his pole, and unless it were shortened it would be higher than any that Sharp-Teeth might erect.

Laderh made it plain that he intended to carry out his threats, and when he shouted that he would kill Sispagut unless the carving was stopped, the Killer-Whale chief thought that the wisest thing to do would be to stop work on the pole. Mind you, he was no coward, but in the wild Northern country it was easy to kill without being discovered, and Sispagut did not want to be the target for a hidden marksmen. He therefore paid Oyai for the carving that had been done and said that he would send for him again.

After several years, Oyai returned to complete the carving, and the pole was named Fin-of-the-Killer-Whale, because at the top was the mascot of Sispagut's clan, Killer-Whale. An elaborate potlatch was planned, and Sispagut decided to go down the river in his dugout canoe to invite Sharp-Teeth and Laderh. As he was approaching Laderh's house, Sispagut began the song of his clan, which, like a school song, was full of boasts about beating the other side.

The song had hardly been started when there was a gunshot and Sispagut fell into his canoe. His wound was not serious, but as a result of the shooting, the erection of the pole and the potlatch party were delayed for a year.

46

This time Sharp-Teeth and Laderh bribed one of Sispagut's nephews to do the shooting, promising that they would make him the next chief. This evil plan succeeded: Sispagut was murdered, but his clan would not accept the chief that Sharp-Teeth had selected. To show that he could not tell them what to do, they erected the Fin-of-the-Killer-Whale totem pole in memory of Sispagut, and for a long time it was the tallest on the river.

Each time Sharp-Teeth and Laderh saw it, they vowed they would get the better of the Killer-Whales. What they did was to form alliances with other clans living in the river country, until their fighting men greatly outnumbered the Killer-Whales'. Then, to prove their superiority, Sharp-Teeth and Laderh announced their intention of erecting a totem pole taller than the Fin-of-the-Killer-Whale.

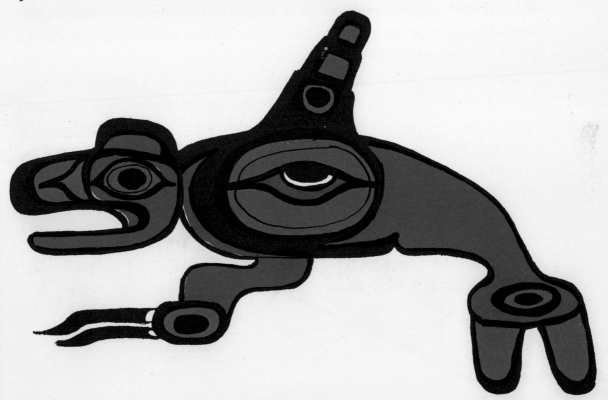

They had to travel nearly a hundred miles to find a red cedar tree of satisfactory height, and then this forest giant — it was more than eighty feet high — had to be towed all the way back to Sharp-Teeth's village.

And Oyai, the master totem-pole carver, was again summoned. He arrived in the autumn, and he was told that the pole must be completed by spring and that it must be more beautiful than any he had ever made. A shelter was built for Oyai, so that even when the weather was bad he could continue to work, and all winter long, from sunrise until dark, Oyai and his assistants carved the pole. Each of the figures was to tell a story of the Eagles or of the Wolf clan, to which Laderh belonged.

The invitations to the potlatch to celebrate the erection of the Eagle-Wolf pole were sent during the winter, and Sharp-Teeth, Laderh, and all their relatives and friends began to prepare for the party. But as the day set for the celebration drew near, Oyai had not yet completed the pole.

Was Oyai working slowly purposely in order to embarrass him, Sharp-Teeth wondered. But when he looked at the pole and saw how beautiful it was, the chief felt that he was being unnecessarily suspicious.

The carving was not quite completed when the first guests arrived. Only on the night before the ceremonies did Oyai put the finishing touches on the pole, and Sharp-Teeth was so well pleased that he paid the artist even more than he had originally promised. In addition to other things, Oyai was given ten white and two black trade blankets, two moose skins, and a gun.

All the plans and the preparations for the party were checked and rechecked, and Sharp-Teeth and Laderh were confident that everything was going to be perfect. But they did not know how hard it would be to get their tall pole to stand upright.

49

Before the guests assembled, Sharp-Teeth's pole was moved so that it lay horizontally in a neatly dug trench that was deepest under the bottom end of the pole. It was the usual system to dig a trench at a slant, so that even before anyone tried to pull up the pole, the top was higher than the bottom.

It was an honor to be given a place on the rope crew, and everyone Sharp-Teeth had appointed was ready to haul away with a right good will. When Sharp-Teeth signaled to begin, singers started a song to which the men pulling the ropes kept time. Sharp-Teeth stood near the pole, watching for the first sign that it was being lifted, but, despite the best efforts of the rope crew, the big pole remained on the ground.

Someone suggested that the position of the ropes be changed, that some should be tied higher and others lower on the pole. While this was being done, the pulling crew rested, and when they tried again, the guests applauded, for the pole started to go up. Quickly, wooden supports were shoved under the pole so that it would not slip back, and each time the pole was raised even by an inch, props were ready to hold it up. But the progress was so slow that at the end of the day the pole still was close to the ground. Everyone was tired and discouraged, but Sharp-Teeth was the most discouraged of all. However, since it was his pole, he tried very hard not to show his disappointment, and his voice sounded cheerful when he said:

"Tomorrow the pole will stand straight up. Now it is time for all of us to stop work and to eat the good things that have been prepared."

All the finest serving dishes and utensils that Sharp-Teeth and Laderh owned or could borrow were brought out. Some of the great wooden dishes were decorated with an Eagle and others with a Wolf, the bird

and animal that were the guardian spirits of Sharp-Teeth's and Laderh's clans. The big dishes were heaped high with food, and the most important guests were given beautiful carved spoons and were invited to help themselves first. Although the celebration program planned for the evening had to be postponed because the pole had not been erected, there was other entertainment that kept everyone amused.

Early next morning, so early that part of the sky was still a wonderful shade of pink and the rest a very light blue, Sharp-Teeth, Laderh, and Oyai, the carver, squatted on the ground near the pole, trying to figure out how it could be pulled up. The ropes were rearranged, and the loose soil that had fallen into the trench was removed, but no one could suggest any method other than the one used the day before. The pulling crew would just have to try again.

When the men and women had taken their places along the ropes, Sharp-Teeth walked along the line saying, "Today you will raise the Eagle into the sky."

51

Then the pulling began, and it went on and on, with everyone straining and puffing. Just when Sharp-Teeth was afraid he never would get his pole up, a ship sailed into the harbor. The captain, who was half-Indian, fired a salute, and then he came ashore. Having watched for a while, he offered to help erect the pole.

Like Captain Roberts, who had assisted Cunneah about a hundred years before, Captain Mattheson brought spare masts, ropes, and other gear to make a derrick for raising the pole. No one minded waiting while the equipment was being set up, because it was interesting to watch, and, furthermore, most of the people had worked hard and welcomed the chance to rest.

It was not until the end of the third day that the pole with the Eagle on top at last stood upright. Then the carved side was turned so that it faced the harbor, and one by one the chiefs who had been invited to the ceremony stepped forward, for each was to have the honor of placing a little soil in the hole around the base of the pole. Many valuable articles — guns, blankets, clothes, even cooking utensils — were thrown into the hole, and then the earth was stamped down hard.

After all this had been done, Sharp-Teeth came out dressed in his ceremonial robes, which were decorated with beads and shells that glittered in the sunlight. He wore a special headdress trimmed with eagle feathers that waved this way and that, as he sang the song of the Eagle clan: ". . . The golden Eagle of the mountains will spread his wings, as he sits above the chiefs on the hilltops." It was a long song, and these words were repeated many times.

After Laderh had sung the Wolf-clan song, Sharp-Teeth began to tell the stories illustrated on the pole.

53

"The giant who sits just below Eagle," said Sharp-Teeth, "is Gyadem-Tso'oyerh (Man-Underneath-the-Ocean), whom my ancestors encountered while traveling from their home in the Far North to the Nass River country. While my people were resting on a beach near the sea, Gyadem-Tso'oyerh popped up through a wave, clutching a huge fish by the tail. His appearance was startling enough, but even more astonishing was what the giant did when he rose from underneath the ocean. He did not try to reach the shore, he did not swim, he just sat on a wave and ate the fish. Having completed his meal, the giant sank into the sea, and no one has ever seen him again."

All the Eagle people knew this tale, for it was one of the famous legends of their clan. But many of the guests had never heard it before, and the figure of Gyadem-Tso'oyerh and the giant fish on the pole made the tale exciting.

Soon after seeing Man-Underneath-the-Ocean, Sharp-Teeth continued, the Eagle people saw another strange creature that looked like a bullhead, a fish that was considered a great delicacy. But the body of this bullhead was covered with human faces. No one would think of eating such a creature, and therefore the bullhead was permitted to swim away.

Although the bullhead and Man-Underneath-the-Ocean were supposed to have been seen only a short time apart, these legends were not illustrated one after another on the pole. Oyai, the carver, put other figures in between, probably because he did not think that two fish, the one eaten by Man-Underneath-the-Ocean and the bullhead with the faces on its body, would make a good design if one were directly over the other. The figures he carved below Man-Underneath-the-Ocean illustrated legends of Laderh's clan, the Wolves, and Laderh now stepped forward to tell them.

54

The most interesting was the one illustrated by the figure with the sharply pointed nose. The story was about a girl named Yaw'l, who had not kept her promise to stay alone in a small cabin in the woods. No one in Yaw'l's family knew that she had broken her pledge, but it was known to some of the creatures of the forest, and they came to punish Yaw'l. These creatures had sharp noses that they used as weapons; they could make their noses as long as they wished and as sharp as knives. One of these sharp-nosed creatures was Wil'Aeq, the Dragonfly, who, while fighting with Yaw'l and her brothers, was killed. And as Dragonfly was dying, it said that all mankind would suffer from its nose. According to Laderh, this threat was made good, because from the sharp nose sprang a host of biting insects.

When it was again Sharp-Teeth's turn to tell stories, he related the adventures of Gunas, who was swallowed by a monster that was half halibut and half eagle. When Oyai illustrated this story, he carved a creature with two heads; one was an eagle's head and the other the head of a fish. About halfway between the two heads he made a figure to show Gunas inside Halibut-Eagle.

The last story illustrated on the pole was about the accident that befell a young man named Aitl. As Sharp-Teeth explained it, Aitl was walking along the beach searching for shellfish, when he met an octopus. (Ordinarily an octopus lives in deep water, but no one interrupted Sharp-Teeth to ask how this one happened to be so near the beach, for such an interruption would have spoiled the story.) The horrible octopus twined its powerful tentacles around Aitl, and while the young man was fighting to free himself, he saw what he thought to be a big rock, and he grabbed hold of it. But it was not a rock; it was a giant clam which clamped Aitl's arm within its shells. Now he was really caught, and no one could rescue him.

You can see Aitl on the pole, with one arm caught by the clam and with the tentacles of the octopus wound around his body.

Why Abraham Lincoln Stands Atop a Pole

THE Eagles were neither more nor less warlike than other Indians who
lived on the Northwest coast. Every tribe took to the warpath when it
was necessary. But the Eagles are remembered as fighters because of a
famous pole that records their war against the Ravens.

The Eagles defeated the Ravens in one battle after another, but the
proud Ravens refused to surrender, and they fled to a small island where
they hoped to be safe from attack, at least for a short time.

Among the Ravens was Metla, a boy of twelve, who had already
earned a reputation for bravery. He was selected to be a lookout and
was assigned to an important post near the tip of the island, where there
fortunately was a big rock behind which he could hide. The channel
between the island and the mainland was narrow, and Metla could look
across the water and see everything that went on in the Eagles' camp;
he had a perfect view of the warriors feasting around the fire.

The cold night wind made Metla shiver, and the longer he watched
the Eagles eating, the hungrier he became. He began to think of how good
it would be to sleep in a warm house and to have as much food as he
wished, but he quickly forgot such thoughts when he saw some of the
warriors leave the campfire and walk to the beach, where their canoes
were lined up. Was the enemy preparing to attack the island? Metla
wondered whether he should immediately run back to warn his people.
Then he thought maybe this was just a trick, and he anxiously waited
and watched.

It seemed a long time to Metla before the Eagle warriors walked away from the canoes and back to the campfire. Actually, the Eagles had had no intention of attacking; their plan was to wait for the Ravens to surrender. The Eagle chief knew that there was no spring on the island to provide drinking water and that the Ravens had very little food.

"When the Ravens suffer the tortures of thirst and when they are weak from lack of food, they will have to give up," said the Eagle chief.

But the Raven clan never did surrender; they escaped. One night while Metla was at his lookout post, he heard a swishing sound that told him a canoe was approaching. Immediately after he had called a challenge, he heard a familiar voice say softly, "I come with good news."

There was only the faintest sound as the messenger landed his canoe on the beach, and then Metla guided him to the Ravens' encampment, where the messenger told of the arrival of a United States government ship.

The homeland of the Eagles and of the Ravens, which we call Alaska, had become a territory of the United States, and the ship brought a company of soldiers who were to patrol the area and enforce law and order.

The Raven leaders quickly decided to leave the island and to ask the Americans for protection. It did not take the Indians long to pack the canoes with their few possessions, and before daybreak the island was completely deserted. The friendly messenger led the way to the Americans' headquarters, and while the Raven leaders went to ask aid of the American commander, the other Indians huddled together on the beach.

The commanding officer of the American garrison could not understand the Indians' language, but when his interpreter told him that the Ravens were fearful of being enslaved, the officer spoke quickly:

"You will always be free."

Then he explained that Abraham Lincoln had decreed by proclamation that in no part of the United States could any human being hold another as a slave. And he read the section of the Constitution which states: "Neither slavery nor involuntary servitude, except as a punishment for crime whereof the party shall have been duly convicted, shall exist within the United States, or any place subject to their jurisdiction."

These words had to be translated from English into the Indians' language, and when the Ravens understood that neither the Eagles or anyone else could ever again make them serve as slaves, they were so happy and grateful that they thanked the commander over and over again.

59

After the Indians had left to tell the wonderful news to the members of their clan, the officer ordered food from the army kitchen sent to the people on the beach, for he knew they were hungry. Much of the white men's food looked and tasted strange to the Indians, but all of them, particularly the girls and boys, thought that never before had anyone had such a fine feast.

Since their villages had been burned, the Ravens had no homes to which they could return, and they asked the commander whether they could build a new village near the fort. He willingly gave permission, and the Indians began to work on log houses close to the Army head-quarters.

Although Metla was big for his age, he did not have enough strength yet to cut trees or to handle the heavy logs of which the houses were built. However, there were many useful things he could do, such as gathering firewood, hunting in the forest for animals and birds, and catching fish. Frequently he brought one of his best fish to the commander, and it was not long before the two became friends. Metla soon learned to speak English, and he also learned much about his white brothers.

After the Ravens were settled in their new village, a peace treaty was signed with the Eagles, and never again did they fight each other. But the war had impoverished the Raven clan to such an extent that it was many years before they could even think of ordering a totem pole. When they did have money enough to hire a carver, they told him that instead of following the usual custom of having their mascot or guardian spirit, the Raven, at the top of the pole, this position of honor was to be given to Abraham Lincoln, the man who had outlawed slavery. But a figure of Raven with outstretched wings was to be carved at the bottom.

60

One of the first gifts that the Army commander had presented to Metla was a picture of Abraham Lincoln, and it was this picture that the totem-pole artist copied when he made his carving. He copied it exactly, even to the tall hat that the great Abraham Lincoln had made famous.

Above is a close-up of the original carving of Abraham Lincoln showing its present worn and weather-beaten condition. At the right is the repaired pole with the later copy of the figure of Lincoln at the top.

61

The pole was given the most prominent position in the village and was called the Proud Raven pole. There it stood for many years, and as long as Metla lived he told and retold its story.

The Proud Raven pole was one of the last big ones erected by the old-time Indians, for after the white settlers came to the Northwest coast, the custom of carving poles was discontinued. Years passed before anyone thought of preserving totem poles, and by that time many of them were in bad condition. Even the Lincoln figure had lost its arms, the brim of the tall hat was missing, and the pole was gray and weather-beaten; all of the paint had been worn off by storms. But the carving had been made so skillfully that it is still a good likeness of the Emancipator.

The pole was repaired by Indian carvers and they made a new figure of Lincoln, which was fastened to the top. The original carving was sent to the Territorial Museum at Juneau, Alaska, where it is exhibited with other things made by the Indians of long ago. The repaired Proud Raven pole was moved to Saxman Totem Park, near Ketchikan, where many other old poles found in deserted Indian villages are now displayed. Visitors from every part of the world travel to see both this group of poles and others preserved in national parks.

Both the United States and the Canadian governments have established special training courses where Indian artists can learn totem-pole carving. Some of the new poles are copies of old ones, and others are carved with completely new designs. When one of these poles is erected there usually is a celebration at which important officials make speeches, just as the chiefs did in the old days, and then refreshments are served. In fact, the celebration is similar to the potlatch of long ago, except that no one is expected to bring presents.

It is good news that the Indians of the Northwest coast are again carving totem poles and so preserving their fascinating and dramatic legends. For we know now that these decorated cedars are to be valued not only because of the stories they tell but also because the Indians' carvings are among the most remarkable works of art produced by any people in the entire world.

Wisconsin State College at Eau Claire
LIBRARY RULES

No book should be taken from the library until it has been properly charged by the librarian.

Books may be kept one week but are not to be renewed without special permission of the librarian.

A fine of two cents a day will be charged for books kept over time.

In case of loss or injury the person borrowing this book will be held responsible for a part or the whole of the value of a new book.

DUE	DUE	DUE	DUE
NOV 18 '64			
NOV 12 '65			
NOV 19 '67			
APR 4 '68			
APR 1 '70			
JUL 14 '71			
NOV 29 '71			
DEC 6 '71			
JUL 21 '72			
FEB 12 '73			